THE
MANAGING U
POCKETBOOK

CW00539672

By Patrick Forsyth

Drawings by Phil Hailstone

"Everything you wanted to know about dealing effectively with your boss, but were afraid to ask."
Steve Hurst, Editor, "Winning Business" magazine

"If your boss is beginning to get to you, read this book to regain your sanity. The emphasis on developing constructive working relationships and a succinct list of do's and don't's will be invaluable for employees and their managers alike."
Richard Chaplin, Executive Editor, "professional marketing" *magazine*

Published by:
Management Pocketbooks Ltd
Laurel House, Station Approach, Alresford, Hants SO24 9JH, U.K.
Tel: +44 (0)1962 735573   Fax: +44 (0)1962 733637
E-mail: sales@pocketbook.co.uk
Website: www.pocketbook.co.uk

This edition published 2002. Reprinted 2004.

© Patrick Forsyth 2002

British Library Cataloguing-in-Publication Data – A catalogue record for this book is available from the British Library.

ISBN 1 870471 98 9

Design, typesetting and graphics by **efex ltd**.   Printed in U.K.

CONTENTS

INTRODUCTION

I don't want any yes-men around me. I want everybody to tell me the truth, even if it costs them their jobs.
Samuel Goldwyn

WISE WORDS

A tricky job
What's the secret of walking on water?
Knowing where the stones are.

THE GOOD, THE BAD & ... YOURS

Your manager may be a nightmare. His/her most constructive comment may be to say *When I want your opinion, I'll give it to you*. Your most flattering comment in reply may be to say that *His/her indecision is final* and when you get a response it may be no more than the ubiquitous *Leave it with me* followed by silence.

Perhaps the first question to ask about your manager is *Can I work for this person?* A poor manager may be a good reason to move on. Here, however, we will take a more constructive line and assume that either in the short term or the long term you are going to work together.

Unless you can influence senior people there is a danger that your job will remain reactive and no more; to some meaningful degree you need to be in the driving seat of the relationship.

INTENTIONS

Your overall intention with regard to your working relationship with senior people, and with your manager in particular, should be the same as for all other aspects of your job. It is to:

- **Do** those things that get you noticed, taken seriously and appreciated

- **Avoid doing** things that lower your reputation, and lead to your suggestions and initiatives being undervalued

- **Tackle effectively** the individual things that need to be done to gain approval, acceptance or agreement to your requests for your job (and for your career)

In this book we consider how to make your relationship with senior people **constructive** and **useful**; and define *managing upwards* as **influencing such people, thus allowing you to do your job more effectively and to get more satisfaction from it.**

A first principle is: first impress, then influence.

DEFINING A MANAGER

Let us be clear. Managers may be concerned with productivity, efficiency, effectiveness, financial measures such as profit or return on sales and more. To be **successful** they must deliver, and to do that they must work at the six key areas of management: planning, organising, recruitment and selection, training and development, motivation and control.

They may need a variety of resources to make this possible, but one factor is common: people.

In simple terms the definition of management is: **the achievement of results <u>through</u> other people**. A manager's greatest asset is therefore his or her people. Managers cannot do everything themselves and they stand or fall by the success of their team. As management guru Peter Drucker said *The basic task of management is to make people productive*.

It is in your manager's interest as much as yours for you to work effectively together; that fact is the starting point to your success in *managing upwards*.

YOUR GREATEST ASSET

Given the role of the manager, a good manager above you can be your greatest asset. They can:

- Help you succeed in your current job
- Develop your competence and skills
- Prepare you for more responsibility
- Specifically help you move on – and up
- Make your working time satisfying, rewarding – even fun

All you have to do is make sure they do.

INTRODUCTION

WHAT YOU WANT OF YOUR MANAGER

Some factors are obvious:

- **Positive**: You want someone fair, clear in communication, who trusts you and is prepared to give responsibility, is good at delegating, good at their own job, decisive, consultative, etc
- **Negative**: you do not want someone secretive, too busy to spend time with you, who doesn't support or trust you; nit-picking at a low level of detail, dictatorial or resistant to change, etc

Some factors are of overriding importance. In many surveys the majority of people say they want their boss to be *someone I learn from*. If a job is not to be endlessly repetitive, then this makes good sense. It leads to change, creativity and new challenges that benefit all – not least the organisation.

Such factors are akin to objectives. Think through what you want to promote as an ideal situation. Then regard influencing matters in the right direction as an *active* process.

INTRODUCTION

WHAT YOUR MANAGER WANTS OF YOU

It's simple: she wants you to do a good job.

You must know what this involves (see also page 16 about job descriptions), and you must appreciate what she thinks makes it possible.

- How self-starting does she want you to be?
- How proactive? How creative?
- What about your time management, productivity, effectiveness and efficiency?
- Does she expect you to be good with people and communication, or to deputise for her on occasion?
- And what does she **not** want? Certainly not to be unnecessarily time-consuming to manage or present particular difficulties.

Think this through and have a clear view in mind. Not sure? The answer is again simple – **ask**. Either when you first work with someone, or perhaps following some change, request a chat to sort things out for you both.

Unless you are clear what you want and what is wanted of you, managing upwards is always going to be akin to fumbling in the dark.

THE BENEFITS OF WORKING EFFECTIVELY TOGETHER

You need to work with senior people in the right way. That means in a way that they *find* they are content with (rather than just the way that they *think* it should be). Thus it should be a way resulting as much from your initiative as from their instruction.

The results are many and worthwhile. For example, they are more likely to:

- Trust you (and check up on you less)
- Consult, listen to and give credence to your ideas
- Delegate to you
- Interfere less (trivial details, for instance)
- Be reasonable (thinking things through with you, rather than just saying *Do this* and attaching the first deadline that comes to mind)
- Support you (in what you do and with others)
- Reward you!

You may be able to add to this list, and target what you particularly want to occur.

Ultimately what works best works for both parties; albeit in different ways.

TESTING WAYS OF WORKING

Different people work in different ways. You need to discover what way of working suits you and your boss as a team. Ask, but also experiment. For example, should you:

- Be enthusiastic about him and his plans?
- Praise him (you like being motivated, after all)?
- Be seen to put the job first?
- Involve him in the social life of the office?
- Keep him informed, be his eyes and ears (but not his spy)?
- Aim to share decision-making?
- Generate ideas (good, practical ones)?
- Offer opinions openly and often (good, considered ones)?

INTRODUCTION

TESTING WAYS OF WORKING

Should you:

- Show you can be trusted (to get things done, to keep a confidence)?
- Only ask for help when it is clearly needed (eg: not twice with the same problem)?
- Get agreements and plans in writing?
- Deal with matters at a formal meeting (which you request) or 'on the run'?
- Discriminate accurately between what is important and less so?
- Take a long-term or short-term view?
- Act as a reminder for him?

The answer to each question needs thinking about. In some cases the answer seems an obvious *yes*, but in others a particular manager may not like or want such an approach.

Adopt a *horses for courses* approach and balance what you want with what they want, and what is possible.

CORPORATE CULTURE

Organisations vary. There may be a culture that favours good relationships where time for consultation, consideration of others, and a creative and group approach are the norm. In the worst kind of culture, secrecy predominates, pressure prohibits consultation and things are generally more difficult.

You may have not a *difficult* boss, but one who is unable to resist a culture that is essentially unconstructive. This leaves you with three options:

- Work to change the system, making it easier for your boss to work with you (maybe a long and difficult struggle)
- Work with your boss, if not to change the system, at least to create an exception (best be open about this and see what the reaction is)
- Work to find a new job (you may conclude that the combination of a difficult boss and an unsympathetic corporate culture is simply incompatible with what you want in your career)

Easy answers cannot be guaranteed. You can, however, adopt a realistic strategy that can pay off longer term.

THE RIGHT RELATIONSHIP

> *I like your qualifications, Gribson – you have the makings of a first class underling.*
> Hector Breeze

(13)

THE RIGHT RELATIONSHIP

A VIRTUOUS CIRCLE

The right working relationship benefits both parties. It is worth making an effort to get it straight, agree it between you and, over time, keep it up to date as things change.

Overall it should be:

- **Straightforward**: you should always know what approach to take, for example what needs prior discussion and what can simply be actioned

- **Open and trusting**: time and effort will be wasted if either party is trying to double guess the other

- **Linked to clear objectives**: common approaches with responsibilities, targets, etc, documented where necessary

THE RIGHT RELATIONSHIP

A VIRTUOUS CIRCLE

- **Well-defined**: this includes a clear definition of the boundaries between jobs, tasks and responsibilities. And clear rules. (Some rules are necessary and should be respected. By all means campaign to change them, but ignoring them or arguing about them causes problems and, worst of all, will mean a manager is less prepared to consult and discuss things that matter more.)
- **Two-way**: the arrangement should set out how both parties operate and interact (not just how you relate to your boss).
- **Mutually beneficial**: in other words it works for both parties, though each may have different agendas and objectives.

A relationship that works encourages more trust and will tend to mean your responsibilities increase. This in turn gives you the opportunity to show what you can do and thus increase the trust ….. _enough!_

THE RIGHT RELATIONSHIP

YOUR JOB DESCRIPTION

You are never going to make what you do impressive if you are not sure what it is you are supposed to be doing. Your job description is not just a formality (necessary only because HR says so). It should be a working tool that acts as an aide memoire for you and your boss. So:

- Make sure that you have a job description
- Check that you agree with what it says
- Ask for clarification about anything that is not clear
- Ensure your boss considers it reflects real life, too
- Review it regularly and make sure it stays up to date

If you are to have a good working relationship with your boss the last thing you want is to have *I didn't think that was my job* type discussions.

Your job description forms a solid foundation from which to make sure that what you do impresses.

THE RIGHT RELATIONSHIP

A SOUND WORKING STRUCTURE

You cannot manage anyone for long in an ad hoc fashion. **You need a sound basis – a routine and a structure**.

This premise is easy to adopt, but then demands two things:

1. **That you think it through**. You need to take the initiative and think about what factors constitute a sound working arrangement. It helps to list them.

2. **That you make it happen**. Again, take the initiative for creating and agreeing the appropriate routine – and making it stick.

Any shortfall here will dilute your efforts to manage upwards; if you cannot get precisely the arrangement you want first time, keep working at it.

THE RIGHT RELATIONSHIP

A SOUND WORKING STRUCTURE

- Adopt a routine, especially regarding how you communicate and how and when you have meetings
- Ensure regular communication (of all sorts, but especially meetings) and get sufficient time together to agree matters between you
- Make sure that project timing is agreed, and particularly that check points or progress meetings are scheduled in advance (by stage if not by date)
- Agree also the nature and style of all the above: for example, what exactly is a progress meeting? How long is it likely to be, should it be preceded by a written report and if so what level of detail is involved?
- Make sure that such practice relates appropriately to tasks (that it is what is needed to get the job done) and to the people (so that both parties feel comfortable with it)
- Address both long- and short-term issues; think about what is needed on a daily basis and also annual matters (like planning or appraisal)

A SOUND WORKING STRUCTURE

Describing a good working methodology is one thing, achieving it is another. Certainly it will not just happen, unless you have an exceptional manager. So you need to be prepared to think it through, and see it as something on which you can take an initiative.

- **Ask**: request the opportunity to discuss it and have some ideas ready. This can be approached overall or, with a less approachable manager, should be tackled over one issue, a project perhaps, initially.

- **Suggest**: put forward ideas, offer suggestions, say what others (chosen because they will be respected) do. Discuss, negotiate, request a test (plead?) – but get something agreed, even if it is a starting point that you return to and refine.

THE RIGHT RELATIONSHIP

A SOUND WORKING STRUCTURE

- **Action**: take the initiative and act assumptively. In other words, just do it.
  For example, as a project starts set out a timetable in writing, scheduling progress
  meetings and send it without comment. Put the date in the diary, send an agenda
  ahead of the time and appear ready for the meeting. Your boss may actually find
  this useful (maybe to the surprise of you both!).

- **Match his or her style**: as you approach this, bear in mind the kind of person your
  boss is. What will be suitable? Aim high by all means but if, ultimately, some
  compromise is likely to be necessary, plan what you might do. For example, attitude
  to detail is important here. Your manager may be a *put it on one page* kind of
  person, or want every *i* dotted, and every *t* crossed. A well-matched case has the
  best chance both of being agreed – and of working.

**Start as you mean to go on, suggest something practical, act to get it agreed and
make it work. Then your boss will want it to continue.**

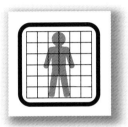

ESTABLISHING A POSITIVE PROFILE

Nothing succeeds like reputation.
John Huston

PERCEPTION IS REALITY

The impression you create matters. It was Oscar Wilde who said *Only shallow people do not judge by appearances*, and you should take note of the principle.

Are you a force to be reckoned with? If you say *I think we should do X*, do your manager and other senior people listen or just say *What would you know about it?* You need to be positive about yourself and you need to cultivate a **professional** image.

What exactly is professional? It is, like beauty, largely in the eye of the beholder. How do your own manager and others view, rate and judge people? You need to think about it and adapt accordingly.

If you hesitate to spend some time and thought on this area, remember this maxim: *If you look like a doormat then, in all likelihood, people will walk all over you.*

ESTABLISHING A POSITIVE PROFILE

KEY OBJECTIVES

There is one important reason to worry about your profile. Your power to influence is directly affected by how you are seen. Your manner, appearance, way of working and how you conduct yourself all contribute to this.

You have some key objectives, including being seen as:

- Competent
- Confident
- Credible

Other factors are important too – being **professional** – but those above are especially relevant to influencing. You need to decide just how to interpret each, given your own situation.

Ensure that you are accepted and respected further up the hierarchy and individual factors will always be easier to achieve.

ESTABLISHING A POSITIVE PROFILE

WHO TO IMPRESS

Be clear about who actually constitutes your **target group**. Think about it. Make a list.
It will probably include:

- Your immediate supervisor or manager
- Their immediate manager
- Other senior people with whom your work involves you (in other departments or functions, perhaps)
- Gatekeepers: a group consisting of those who prevent or allow easy access to others (such as a secretary or assistant)
- Communicators: a group who can communicate news or opinion about you (these may range from the office gossip to whoever runs an internal newsletter)

Some may interact with you a good deal, others may be worth forging stronger links with. All are in a position to influence how your boss will work with you because his or her opinion of you comes, in part, from these people.

**Make sure that messages passed back are positive and as you would wish them.
Use these channels actively.**

ESTABLISHING A POSITIVE PROFILE

THE RIGHT IMAGE

This is something you should define. What qualities must be in evidence before you are seen as professional? You probably want to be seen as:

Reliable, interested in what you do, responsible, experienced, expert, discreet, thorough, careful, creative, a good communicator, approachable, well prepared and organised.

You might also, depending on the organisational culture, want to be thought respectful or ethical.

These qualities can be grouped in three categories:

- Your inherent qualities, those that shine through and need no great attention
- Qualities that need strengthening (eg: if being a good communicator is important, maybe the first step is to improve your report writing style)
- Qualities that can benefit from some, what is the right word – *exaggeration?*

In other words, **making people aware of how you operate and what you have to offer is an *active* process.**

THE RIGHT IMAGE

Two additional points:

- One caveat: do not overdo things. You do not want a reputation for being unpleasantly *pushy*. But this is not what is meant here. For example, you might decide that being *seen* as someone who gives attention to detail is important (maybe with certain people or projects). The way to do this is not to say so, it is to *show* it. If this goes beyond your natural tendencies then you may need to enhance the ability and exaggerate it somewhat.

- Finally, you might also list and work on characteristics that you should avoid and *be seen not to embrace*. For example, few managers appreciate time wasters, whingers or people who spend half their office life engaged in office politics or on the internet.

WORKING TO CREATE IMPACT

*Anyone can do any amount of work, provided
it isn't the work he is supposed to be doing at the moment.*
Robert Benchley

THE RIGHT TARGETS

To establish and maintain a good working relationship with your manager you have to be effective – and to be effective you need to aim at the right things. This means:

- Being clear about your aims and responsibilities (the comments about job descriptions earlier are relevant here)
- Understanding – and hitting – specific targets that may be part of your remit (never underestimate the importance of this)
- Delivering – doing what is expected of you (doing more than is expected has even more impact)
- Your performance being trouble free, and being noticed (your boss should be aware not only that you have succeeded, but of the details: for example, that a project was on time despite unexpected problems, that you carried other people with you)

Never confuse activity with achievement. No manager will be impressed, or easier to deal with, just because they know you are *busy* – it is results that matter (not least because your results reflect on your manager).

WORKING TO CREATE IMPACT

WHAT YOU DO AND HOW YOU DO IT

Sometimes managers seem to notice **nothing**. Ultimately, however, achieving goals does have impact. So too do the ways in which you work. For example, normally it pays to:

- Be thorough, with all the details accommodated and no loose ends

- Be consistent and reliable, so that you get a reputation for **delivering** (this alone can put you at the front of the queue when interesting, and important, projects are allocated)

- Match with your manager, reflecting his or her requirements and concerns while adding in your own

- Have the right attitude (it is probably best to be interested, even enthusiastic, about most things. Though you do not want to become a dumping ground for unwanted work – *Patrick never complains* – so a balance is necessary)

But whatever else, **enthusiasm is infectious!**

WORKING TO CREATE IMPACT

DELIVERING

THE ESSENTIALS

Three things are of overriding importance if your work is to impress. It should be:

- **On spec**: the first thing to deliver is **exactly what was agreed or asked for**. If there is a difference it should only be a positive one (but even that might collect a reprimand if other things were more important)

- **On time**: ensure you meet any deadline, provided it is agreed and possible. (Never be railroaded into agreeing impossible deadlines; the only response to your saying – *I told you it was insufficient time* – will be the reply *Then you shouldn't have agreed the date*. Yes, unreasonable, but real life.)

- **On budget**: money matters more than many things in organisational life. Try not to get into a position where agreed budgets are exceeded (or planned cost reductions missed). Creating pleasant surprises in this area will be noticed, but beware of setting precedents

Do this, and do it consistently, and any manager is going to regard you as someone worth noticing.

DELIVERING

CREATING A BALANCE

Linking to the previous page, it is worth bearing in mind a juggling act that applies to many things. Imagine, in the chart shown below, that the lines are elastic.

The three elements – time, quality and cost – may always be a compromise; for example, spend less and quality is reduced (as it says in one American management book – *they didn't want it right, they wanted it Wednesday*).

Get the balance right – something else to ask about and agree perhaps – and the outcome of what you do will be more secure.

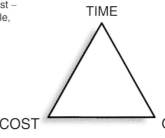

DOING YOUR HOMEWORK

If you fail because of lack of thought or effort then you have only yourself to blame. You must:

- Do the necessary groundwork. Check facts and figures, consider the details, do any research that enables you to complete the task satisfactorily

- Ask others where necessary (this can be informal – a good networking system helps everyone)

- Ask your manager for any necessary support. If she has to be involved at some stage, or needs to give permission for you to access files or set up discussions with people who are *her* colleagues – get that organised

Experience changes things. If you fail to ask for support or talk to the right person the project may fail. Get it right and not only is the project successful, but next time you will be that much more self-sufficient.

Running before you can walk or with the wrong shoes can only trip you up. Organise yourself to be successful.

A GOOD IDEA

Managers are not paid to **have** all the good ideas that keep their department (company or whatever) running successfully. They are paid to **make sure there are enough good ideas available to do just that**. Where do the ideas come from? Sensible managers will regard their people as the best source of ideas.

If you are someone who does generate ideas, if you can be relied upon not only to contribute when asked, but to take a lead – this can only help increase your influence. So:

- Think through all aspects of a suggestion (to the extent of doing any research or checking that may entail)
- Consider the best way to present your idea. Will a chance remark do? Should you introduce it in a meeting (where others may lay claim to it)? Does it need a written note?
- Be prepared for rejection. However creative you are not every idea will be right or possible to implement (and this may well be because of facts outside your knowledge). But the only way to get some ideas accepted is to stick your neck out.

The only way to get a nil rejection rate is never to put forward ideas; and this is not the way forward. In most jobs an element of creativity is essential to success.

ENHANCING IMPACT

Beyond delivering (with a capital D), you should also:

- Undertake some internal public relations – albeit judiciously – to tell people that you are effective
- Associate yourself with success (e.g: associate with successful people, perhaps more senior and certainly not with the office gossip or troublemaker)
- Use success to secure new challenges, not just asking to be involved but quoting other experiences – *Now that I have ... an involvement with X makes sense*
- Be generous to others you work with; claiming *all* the credit when manifestly others contributed is rarely acceptable

The combined effects of such strategies may improve your standing sufficiently for you to achieve more of what you want.

(34)

COMMUNICATING
WITH SENIOR PEOPLE

The world is divided into people who do things – and people who get the credit.
Dwight Morrow

COMMUNICATING WITH SENIOR PEOPLE

THE BASICS

Fact: Organisations have hierarchies and they do mean something.
The trend may be towards flatter organisation structures and
more informal styles, but senior people are, well, senior.
There is something of a balancing act to be done
therefore, and you need to:

- Cultivate friendly relationships
- Maintain an appropriate degree of
  respect and distance
- Create a good working relationship
  with people (almost every aspect of
  this book comes back to this)

**Balance respect with involvement to
create appropriate positioning
on the hierarchical ladder.**

COMMUNICATING WITH SENIOR PEOPLE

THE BASICS

Assuming that you are relating to people in the right sort of way, another important factor is **timing**. Consider two different possibilities:

1. They communicate with you.
One philosophy follows the old adage that if a senior person says *Jump!* the only response is *How high?* But is this always right and do senior people always expect it?

There are certainly occasions when the right reaction to a *summons* is to stall. You may want to finish something more important (or let them decide which is most important) or to have time to prepare for whatever the discussion will be about.

So, be prepared to stand up for yourself; be polite but be prepared to be firm (you may not always succeed, but you may achieve a surprisingly good rate of strike).

THE BASICS

2. You communicate with them. In which case the rule is clear: always choose your moment carefully.
Again, there is a balance to be struck. Insist too much – *But I must see you today!* – and, if he agrees, you may find that you have given yourself a very difficult meeting (time is short and his mind is on other things). Leave things too long and the moment passes, the project has run on too long or, perhaps worst of all, the problem has got bigger. In the latter case you are on a hiding to nothing. Saying *But I've been trying to get to see you for days* will only make matters worse.

A good moment
Conversely, when you have his full attention, when he feels the meeting (or any other form of communication for that matter) is necessary, appropriately set up and likely to fit in with other things he is doing – then you are more likely to get a good hearing.

But, be realistic. Offices are busy places. You might want an hour with someone, but is this likely to be agreed or if it is will it be resented? Compromise if necessary, but make the compromise work.

THE BASICS

So:

- **Consider timing carefully**. Even in small ways timing always needs thinking about. Do you interrupt that meeting, stop her on her way out of the office or set a special session?

- **Plan and schedule ahead as far as possible.**

- **Stick to time**. Always be on time for meetings. Always set a start and finish time for meetings you set or request. And give reasonable notice whenever possible. Some things are inevitably emergencies; but do not cry wolf. (Again, little things can be important. If your every e-mail carries a priority symbol it may quickly annoy and will certainly be ineffective).

COMMUNICATING WITH SENIOR PEOPLE

GETTING THE MOST FROM MEETINGS

Meetings are much maligned (*Meetings are indispensable when you don't want to do anything:* J. K. Galbraith), but many are necessary. If you *work* them well they can play a prime part in allowing you to influence events. Certain things are important:

- **Prepare**: read papers circulated in advance, note the agenda, think about what you want to say
- **Look the part**: especially in terms of being well organised
- **Clarify**: never participate in discussions if you are not clear about the objectives – ask for clarification (there is no harm in being seen to have things straight before making comments)
- **Handle the discussion**: for example, judge when to speak and when not
- **Communicate effectively**: preparation helps, but in a meeting, with time pressing, it is important to be precise and concise and, above all, clear

COMMUNICATING WITH SENIOR PEOPLE

GETTING THE MOST FROM MEETINGS

- Obey the rules: be on time, respect the Chair, observe any formalities and conduct yourself reasonably and courteously
- Read between the lines: people's motivation may be disguised (or their intentions negative or destructive) so watch out for any politics
- Display some clout: be prepared to fight your corner, dig your heels in or challenge others and do so confidently, with a well argued and well supported case
- Maintain flexibility: be prepared, but not locked into a position – meetings are a forum in which you must be quick on your feet
- Make clear notes: always be sure you know what has been said, what has been decided, and what action is required of you
- Follow up: act upon matters agreed, as agreed (you do not want to be the one shown up at the next meeting as failing to implement action points)

There are skills to develop here. *Meetings can be a stage on which much of your upward management can be played out successfully – use them wisely and carefully.

* Maybe you should also read *The Meetings Pocketbook*

COMMUNICATING WITH SENIOR PEOPLE

LISTENING

Senior people do not want misunderstandings. They do not want to hear *I'm not quite sure what you meant* … and they do not want any confusion resulting from their contact with you to waste any of **their** time.

As a result it is important to:

- Listen: really listen (see checklist on pages 43-46)
- Ask, if in doubt: and do so immediately (going back at the end of a meeting and querying something casts doubt on your total understanding)
- Recap if necessary: a quick statement – *so this means that* … can clarify rapidly and is noticed as nothing except being sure
- Make notes: develop the habit of doing so quickly and accurately (and maybe checking them **immediately** after a discussion, filling them out somewhat while things are fresh in your mind)

Few skills are so appreciated by senior people. If you listen to get things right and get them right first time – your ability to influence is automatically enhanced.

LISTENING CHECKLIST

Make listening an *active process*. The checklist shows how. You should:

- **Want to listen**: this is easy once you realise how useful it is to the communication process

- **Look like a good listener**: staff will appreciate it and feedback will be more forthcoming if they see they have your attention

- **Understand**: it is not just the words but the meaning that lies behind them you must note

- **React**: let people see that you have heard, understood and are interested. Nods, small gestures and signs and comments will encourage the other person's confidence and participation – *right?*

43

COMMUNICATING WITH SENIOR PEOPLE

LISTENING CHECKLIST

- **Stop talking**: other than small acknowledgements, you cannot talk and listen at the same time. Do not interrupt
- **Use empathy**: put yourself in the other person's shoes and make sure you really appreciate their point of view
- **Check**: if necessary, ask questions promptly to clarify matters as the conversation proceeds. An understanding based even partly on guesses or assumptions is dangerous. But ask questions diplomatically, do not say *You didn't explain that properly*
- **Remain unemotional**: too much thinking ahead – *however can I overcome that point?* – can distract you
- **Concentrate**: allow nothing to distract you
- **Look at the other person**: nothing is read more rapidly as lack of interest than an inadequate focus of attention

COMMUNICATING WITH SENIOR PEOPLE

LISTENING CHECKLIST

- **Note particularly key points**: edit what you hear so that you can better retain key points manageably
- **Avoid personalities**: do not let your view of a member of staff distract you from the message
- **Do not lose yourself in subsequent arguments**: some thinking ahead may be useful; too much and you suddenly may find you have missed something
- **Avoid negatives**: to begin with clear signs of disagreement (even a dismissive look) can make the other person clam up and destroy the dialogue
- **Make notes**: do not trust your memory and, if it is polite to do so, ask permission before writing comments down

Listening successfully is a practical necessity if you are to excel at communicating with your people.

MAKE THEM LISTEN TO YOU

Apart from having something worthwhile and interesting to say, and making sure that you do not distract (by being obtuse or verbose for instance), here is a true golden rule:

Never try to compete with an interruption.

You may be in full flight – your pet proposal is going over a storm – but, whatever may interrupt, **always** pause. It may be the telephone, a visitor, or the office tea lady on her rounds. It may even just be a moment's apparent distraction for no obvious reason. Whatever it is:

- Pause at once
- Acknowledge what you are doing – *I'll just wait while*… and do so assumptively as if it is as much in their best interests as yours
- If necessary (for example when the interruption persists – eg: an unscheduled visitor stays on, and on) suggest an alternative time (but get something specific agreed: *Let's meet again at 3 pm* not just later)
- Recap as you restart and be sure that nothing has been missed

No communication will impress if only a part of it is actually heard.

BE ASSERTIVE

Alongside persuasion, you also need to adopt an assertive approach and make it acceptable. Be careful not to be too strident (it can give the wrong signals, eg: desperation), otherwise:

- **Have the courage of your convictions**: only a well prepared case can be presented this way
- **Stick to your ground when challenged**: and back up what you say with facts
- **Avoid circumspection**: do not say *perhaps we should …* when you mean *we should certainly …*
- **Use tone and manner to reinforce your intention**: look and sound as if you mean business
- **Do not be put off with bluster**: treat a smokescreen as exactly that
- **Keep any argument objective and businesslike**: avoid emotional pleas or reactions

Being assertive only means adopting a planned, positive way of putting over a strong case. Senior people will expect and respect it.

NOTES

GETTING YOUR BOSS TO AGREE

When I am getting ready to reason with a man, I spend one third of my time thinking about myself and what I am going to say; and two thirds thinking about him and what he is going to say.
Abraham Lincoln

GETTING YOUR BOSS TO AGREE

TWO KEY PRINCIPLES

The way to get what you want may be just to ask. If the request is sensible, the result likely to be useful and the relationship with your manager good, then this may be sufficient. If not, remember two things as a preliminary to everything else you do:

- Do not just ask, *persuade*
- Do not give up, *persist*

Persuasion requires particular skills (investigated over the next few pages). Persistence at least is easy (though do not become a complete bore) and it should never be underrated – as just one more attempt may be the successful one.

Think about being persistent, go on think about it, I really want you to, go on do it – read the next page (then I'll stop insisting).

GETTING YOUR BOSS TO AGREE

PERSISTENCE

The difficulties here are largely psychological. It is difficult when you have been put off several times *(Leave it for the moment – I can't do anything until after the budget period ends – She's in a meeting)* to raise something again. So:

- Continue contact until you are firmly told *No* and take everything else at face value (eg: if you are told *after the month end*, assume it means just that)
- Try different methods – send a note, then telephone, then raise it at a meeting
- Remember that some methods are better reminders than others (a telephone call can be forgotten in a short time and an e-mail can be deleted in a second)
- Find a creative approach if possible

Sometimes you need to make multiple contacts over a comparatively short period, at other times you need patience and a resolution to raise the issue at the right moment.

UNDERSTANDING DECISION-MAKING

What happens when you ask your manager to agree to something? Assuming he considers the request, then it helps to understand the way his mind works. Effectively people move through several stages of thinking, thus:

- **I matter most**. Whatever you want me to do, I expect you to worry about how I feel about it, respect me and consider my needs

- **What are the merits and implications of the case you make?** Tell me what you suggest and why it makes sense (the pluses) and whether it has any snags (the minuses) so that I can weigh it up; bearing in mind that few, if any, propositions are perfect

UNDERSTANDING DECISION-MAKING

- **How will it work?** Here people additionally want to assess the details, not so much about the proposition itself but about the areas associated with it. For example, you might want agreement to become involved with a project. The idea of the project might appeal, but if it clashes with something else important the clash might appear to be a minus. If the case is finely balanced, it could be rejected because of that.

- **What do I do?** In other words what action – exactly – is now necessary? This too forms part of the balance. Why, for example, did you buy this book? Did you have a quick flick through and spot something you thought might be helpful? In deciding to buy it, you recognised (and accepted) that you would have to read it and that this would take a little time. The action – reading – is inherent in the proposition and, if you were not prepared to take it on, this might have changed your decision.

UNDERSTANDING DECISION-MAKING

It is when this thinking is complete that people will feel they have sufficient evidence with which to make a decision. They know the pluses and minuses, and can compare these with those of any other options. Remember that your suggestions often relate to other things; if a cost is involved, for instance, on what else might the money be spent? Remember too, some choices are close run, with one option only just coming out ahead of others.

This thinking process enables a decision to be made; and allows the person to feel that the decision reached is both sensible and considered.

GETTING YOUR BOSS TO AGREE

PERSUASION'S MAGIC FORMULA

People do not agree to ideas or plans, they sign up to the results of actions or ideas. The key concept to use here differentiates between what are called **features** and **benefits**:

- **Features** are the factual elements of something
- **Benefits** are what it does or means to someone

A crucial factor in achieving agreement is in **talking benefits**. You need to spell out the advantages in specific terms, leading with benefits, stressing those benefits which make the strongest case and using features to back up the argument.

PERSUASION'S MAGIC FORMULA

Because this concept is so important, let us look at an example.

Imagine wanting to change a system of some sort (details do not matter). You are sure what you have planned is an improvement. It is less complicated, it can be computerised (rather than being done manually), it is flexible and simple to administer.

Are these factors features or benefits?

They are all features. What does *being less complicated* mean? (It might mean less thorough.) How does running the system on a computer help? What does *flexible* mean, for goodness sake? A useful umbrella term perhaps, but it needs spelling out. Even good-sounding words like *simple* fail to do the case justice.

If 'simple' means that it can be implemented at lower cost by a lower level of staff, saving money and freeing up other people for more important tasks – that needs saying.

Benefits come first, **features** demonstrate how benefits are possible.

GETTING YOUR BOSS TO AGREE

PERSUASION'S MAGIC FORMULA

Benefits come in various forms so, in searching for points to strengthen a case, look for benefits:

- **To your manager in her work capacity**: a benefit would be something that improves the productivity of the department
- **To your manager as an individual**: here a benefit might be something that makes life easier, reduces worry, or gives her more time
- **To other people (with whom your manager is concerned)**: this might mean something that affects her own boss or others in the organisation.

These are not mutually exclusive. You can look for and use a *package* of benefits from all the above categories.

Select the right benefits, describe them clearly and you have the basis of a strong case. This makes agreement more likely.

GETTING YOUR BOSS TO AGREE

ADDED WEIGHT

Two factors can be used to add additional weight to your argument:

1. **Proof**: that is any evidence **other than** what you say, eg: someone else's opinion, the results of a test or trial, figures where appropriate – all add weight to the argument from a different perspective and make the time and effort of assembling them worthwhile.

2. **Thoroughness**: and this is meant in the broadest sense. An argument carries more weight when your manner is appropriate. When, manifestly, you have done your homework, when accompanying facts and figures are well explained, and when the way it is put over shows good preparation and presentation. For example, the quality of a presentation or report (memo, etc) may condition the response. A reaction may begin and end as *What a rotten presentation, it's obviously a stupid idea.*

Always do justice to your requests, and give your argument suitable weight.

GETTING YOUR BOSS TO AGREE

SPECIFIC REQUESTS
MORE PAY

Some do's and don't's:

Do not say:
I've been working very hard,
I have been here a long time,
X gets more money so I should too

Do not quote a friend in another organisation
and never plead poverty due to personal
circumstances that have nothing to do with
work (*I'm moving house*). Also, do not
threaten, demand or become emotional.

SPECIFIC REQUESTS

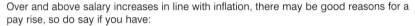

MORE PAY

Over and above salary increases in line with inflation, there may be good reasons for a pay rise, so do say if you have:

- Increased your responsibilities
- Saved the organisation money
- Achieved new qualifications or skills
- Increased your contribution (eg: with ideas)
- Exceeded expectations or targets

Or if you are having to:

- Work longer or more unsociable hours
- Travel or stay away more

Fit with the review processes where possible, but whenever you need to push do so confidently and assertively (the worst answer is perhaps *No*, in which case plan when you can best ask again).

Be objective, be factual – and stay calm.

Note: a creative approach might work. In an idle moment a boss of mine once told me he had obtained a rise by saying he would have to work harder that year as it was a leap year. I waited nearly three years until the next one to remind him – and got a small, extra, increase as a result!

SPECIFIC REQUESTS

MORE RESPONSIBILITY/PROMOTION

There are two routes ahead. First, responsibility can be added piece by piece until the whole job is rather different. At that point changes may need formalising. Secondly, one can move straight to a significant change – a step up.

Both are integral parts of active career management. The piece by piece route is helped by such interim approaches as encouraging delegation and taking initiatives.

To get things formalised, the best approach is similar to asking for more money: it should be objectively and factually based. Do not use emotion: *but I've been here three years!*

Just one other thing to keep in mind. Most organisations are concerned about fairness (because it's, well, fair – and unfairnesses on staff matters can all too easily overlap into employment legislation. So, while you should not demand because of this, a need to be fair may appropriately be part of a reasoned argument).

GETTING YOUR BOSS TO AGREE

SPECIFIC REQUESTS

TRAINING AND DEVELOPMENT

Training is generally seen as a good thing, but restraints on time and money may interfere. An old maxim quotes a manager saying: *What if I invest time and money training my people, and they leave?* The answer is another question: *What happens if you don't train them – and they stay?*

So, key ways to make your training suggestions acceptable include:

- Stressing the benefits – the way you will be able to perform your job after training (be as specific as possible)
- Focusing on results (not just *I will be able to write better reports*, but *My reports will do a better job for the department*, spelling out how)
- Being practical: it is inherently more difficult to organise a month away than a couple of days at a seminar
- Offering proof (eg: benefits experienced by others) and utilising the support of others where appropriate (the training manager, perhaps)
- Mixing the topics of training – some specific and task-based, others perhaps more career-focused

DEALING WITH DIFFICULTIES

There is always a well known solution to every human problem –
neat, plausible … and wrong.
H. L. Menkin

THE BOSS FROM HELL

Bosses come in every shape, size and sort. Let us hope that yours is not irredeemable, but – like most – he or she probably has some characteristics that make for some difficulty. Over the next few pages we look at some common problems.

First, consider some general points:

- Identify the problem and try to ascertain **why** it is occurring (perhaps just ask?)
- Do not over-react, especially with visible irritation
- Plan your response and, if necessary, see it as a campaign and do not aim for an *instant fix* (which may not be possible)
- Approach it sensitively and use all your communications skills

Remember bulls in china shops usually cause more damage than anything else – softly, softly may be the (only) way.

DEALING WITH DIFFICULTIES

COMMUNICATION HELPS!

Never automatically assume things are complicated. Sometimes, problems are caused by sheer ignorance. Something is done unthinkingly, or for good, though ultimately inappropriate, reasons and can be corrected very easily. How? **You just ask**.

Example: I remember receiving regular information from my boss. It was necessary and allowed me to complete a task I enjoyed. But its form necessitated some sorting out. My boss had never asked how the information should be provided, and it subsequently turned out that he honestly felt it was ideal.

The answer? A simple request – *I wonder if you could …* backed with an example of how it could be better arranged, and a brief explanation about how that would save time – received instant agreement. A permanent change in practice (no additional effort was necessary to produce the information in the revised form) followed.

If it is not a problem, do not treat it like a problem (just make it easy to agree a change).

THE BOSS WHO IS SECRETIVE

First, accept that there are things that your manager knows that you do not, because it is inappropriate or unimportant to inform you (you could probably spend all day just exchanging details, after all).

If there **is** a habit you need to try to change, resist the temptation to gripe or complain vaguely. Rather:

- **Be specific**: discuss particular things where your non-involvement has caused problems
- **Gather evidence**: show why it affects you (other than being irritating) and what results from it
- **Emphasise the plus side**: spell out the advantages of more openness, suggesting *improved information flow*, rather than *stopping being secretive*
- **Involve others**: as such a habit may affect others similarly, get everyone to engage in the same sort of action to rub in the message

Finally, do *not* respond in kind and be secretive yourself; your good example may help.

THE BOSS WHO WILL NOT DELEGATE

Why not? There are many reasons (beyond sheer cussedness!) why a manager may be bad at delegation. Discovering *why* may prove the first step to changing matters. Major reasons include:

- Fear that the process is time consuming (demonstrate that you can pick things up and take over fast)

- Fear that something will go wrong and he will be blamed (trust may remove this in time)

- Fear that you will do something *better* than him (well, so you might, perhaps you should describe it as being done differently rather than better)

- Hanging on to things which, although appropriate to delegate, he *likes* doing (find him something else more important or even more satisfying to do)

Discovering the reasons and dealing with them is more likely to change things than just a general complaint.

THE BOSS WHO INTERFERES

This is a sign of the control freak and usually goes along with an inability to delegate. The only antidote is to **build up your boss's confidence in you**, showing that all *does* go well even without their monitoring every moment.

Specifically:

- Supply progress reports or arrange discussions ahead of being asked
- Create regular continuity of contact; gaps will simply encourage unnecessary contacts
- Work to a plan you can describe (this says not only that all is well, but that it will continue to be so)
- Stick to the brief (later you can try to make changes, once the confidence in you is there)
- Deal with checks objectively and factually and do not let your irritation show
- Be sure that you can **always** quote chapter and verse on what is happening **at any time**

And be patient – this needs a campaign to cure it.

THE BOSS WHO RESISTS CHANGE

Again, it helps if you can work out **why** this is occurring. If it is one major thing you may be able to tackle it. Maybe she is frightened of new technology (a problem often made worse by having younger staff who are not). If so, you might be able to help (pick something straightforward you know is a problem and offer help; you might even become a source of regular help).

Maybe she is just busy, stubborn or old fashioned, reacting against anything that upsets her existing ways, in which case other methods are needed.

Do not fight your boss, you will add stubbornness to resistance – work *with* her.

THE BOSS WHO RESISTS CHANGE

Three particular tactics may help here:

1. In making suggestions, **separate the process of change from the results of making the change**. Often what is feared or resented is just the inconvenience of making the change – sell the results (benefits) and reactions may be different; minimise the hassle and the case is stronger still

2. **Assist – indeed, enliven – imagination**. Describe **how** it will be after a change and paint an attractive and truly descriptive picture

3. **Do the groundwork.** Make agreeing the change consist of saying yes to the results, not yes to a difficult process of sorting everything out

All three points make getting agreement easier. Afterwards (thinking of next time) do not try to take all the credit – even if it is rightfully yours! If your boss made a good decision, it does no harm to say so. You are a team, right?

Twas ever thus: *Change is not made without inconvenience, even from worse to better.*
Samuel Johnson (1709-1784)

THE BOSS WHO IS RUDE/ABRUPT

Rudeness may be intractable; if so, you may decide to learn to live with it, and assume no great harm is intended. Or its impact may be unintentional, or at least something that your manager is unaware hurts to the extent it does. If so then a simple request may suffice to prompt a change.

If not, then you have to mount a campaign. For example:

● Set a good example with your courtesies to other people (and prompt your boss also where possible, eg: drafting a thank you letter for him to sign)

● Refer to behaviour linked to other people (*I know Mary's secretary really hates being called that – if you used her proper name, I'm sure we'd get more co-operation*)

DEALING WITH DIFFICULTIES

THE BOSS WHO IS RUDE/ABRUPT

- Ask advice about related matters (*How do you think I can approach John about that without offending him?*)
- Ignore the rudeness, then make it clear what you are doing (*Sorry, I was sure you weren't talking to me like that*)

If you wear him down in this way, he should eventually take the hint (he may even say *thank you!*).

Note: if the upset is *intended*, the same tactics may work. In bad cases you need to check why it is happening. For example, it could be an alternative to meeting some issue head on or signs of a deep incompatibility that makes you need to consider your future.

THE BOSS WHO SAYS *LEAVE IT WITH ME*

The phrase *leave it with me* is a favourite, apparently helpful, but frequently you never hear another word on the subject. The solution is often straightforward:

- Always ask for (better still, suggest), and then agree, a follow up date so that you can check for information on that date rather than having to wait for your boss to mention it to you

- Make this sound convenient to him rather than you (*To save you time, why not let me…*)

- Stress the benefits. Do not over-emphasise **your** situation, make a point of showing how compliance assists him

THE BOSS WHO SAYS *LEAVE IT WITH ME*

- Do not let it lie. If no answer is forthcoming on the due date, then set another (and, if necessary, another). Be persistent and try to link things to other timing (eg: *Let me check with you on 25th, we should have things sorted out before the end of the month, don't you think?*)

- It may help to offer to get involved and take on part of any task involved (eg: *Why don't I get the figures out, then all you have to do is … and by 25th it should all be settled*)

- If you really need more ammunition, then consider making it public by referring to other people who are/seem aware of the delay (eg: *I told John I could start X once I have this out of the way*)

With the worst examples of this the key is **persistence**. Knowing you will not forget or give up your reasonable approach should wear him down.

THE BOSS WHO NEVER CONSULTS

The problem here can be similar to non-delegation (fear, for instance – see page 67).

The solution is to demonstrate how useful consultation can be, to your manager and to the operation. Yet it takes some time, and in a busy – pressurised – life this may be seen as a major problem.

You need to persuade her of the concept of investing time **now**, in order to save time later. You can start in small ways. And you can start by taking the initiative rather than just requesting that **she** consult.

DEALING WITH DIFFICULTIES

THE BOSS WHO NEVER CONSULTS

So:

- Ask – *Can we take five minutes? I think it would be useful if I understood …*
- Tell – *One possible problem with this new project is X, I've got a way round that, I think. Can we discuss it for a few minutes (there may be other ways I could help)?*
- Demonstrate – if there are numbers of people involved report on the benefits of your consultations with others (down the line, perhaps)
- Consult with others – *I had a chat with James about X. It was very useful, but you are really the prime mover here; maybe we should …*
- Use small successes to build the habit. Show how well one thing worked and sell the benefits of 'more of the same'

If you are an effective person (would you be reading this if not?) consultation **will** be useful. **The trick is to get started and demonstrate the benefits so that your boss will want to use it more.**

DEALING WITH DIFFICULTIES

COVER UP

What do you do if your boss asks you to cover up for him? It might be work or private (eg: the kind of subterfuge involved in hiding an affair). Leaving the odd white lie aside, for most people **not** being involved in such things is only right. Bad cases need addressing head on:

- Raise the issue formally and explain how uncomfortable it makes you
- Suggest, if possible, another way *(If she never telephoned the office, I would know nothing about it)*
- Stick to your objective of not being involved and do not moralise
- Most people recognise that this sort of thing is wrong and agreement to avoid it should be attainable. If not, then consider whether in the long term you want to work for such a person
- Really serious whistle-blowing incidents go beyond the scope of this book. (Suffice to say that you should proceed with caution, take advice from someone who can be objective about the matter, and consider acting only in a way that keeps your involvement confidential)

DEALING WITH DIFFICULTIES

BIG PROBLEMS

There are interpersonal problems that negate the whole boss/subordinate relationship. Such include bullying, sexual harassment, or racial (or other) discrimination from your boss; all must be addressed very seriously.

- First, check – and check very carefully – that your worst fears are true and that what is happening cannot be a misunderstanding. Keep an open mind while you do so and involve your organisation's consultation processes as necessary

BIG PROBLEMS

- Secondly, consider carefully what you want to do. There are various options, ranging from organising for someone else (maybe your boss's boss) to intervene, to taking legal action; or just walking away. You have to balance what should be done with the practicalities, and include a longer-term career view in your thinking. It is not suggested that you put up with anything of so serious a nature; equally, if you see that your situation can never be the same again, you may want to organise a fall-back position ahead of taking action.

The legal implications are beyond the scope of this book, though it should be acknowledged that there are legal implications (and if you experience such problems you should seek sensible advice, early on, from a union, a staff association or similar).

Always address such issues, always consider what you do carefully, always take formal advice and do not allow yourself to feel isolated and alone.

CREATING BIG PROBLEMS

Some big problems you can create. So here, with no apology if they are obvious, are some real no-no's that can lead to potentially **big and lasting** problems.

- Never bribe or blackmail your manager (with favours of any sort)
- Never make important requests in a social setting (particularly not if the whole department has been in the pub for hours and the answer to almost anything would be yes)
- Never attempt to persuade her in difficult, perhaps contrived, circumstances (eg: in a meeting with her manager – floating an idea that you have primed the senior person to approve, perhaps)
- Never exert emotional pressure (by bursting into tears, say)
- Never lie to bolster a case (you make your chances of being believed again minimal)

Think before you take what seems like an easy fix. If it seems too easy, there is probably a catch – and it could come back to haunt you.

DEALING WITH DIFFICULTIES

IF ALL ELSE FAILS

You should always bear human nature in mind. Many of the suggestions for dealing with difficulties involve a soft approach. Saving face, bolstering confidence, making safe, and sheer tact all have a part to play. If you think diplomacy is another word for sledgehammer then hold yourself in check. Only rarely, and with great care, is a display of out and out anger (controlled) appropriate.

Beyond that there is one other tactic that has not been mentioned: a little old fashioned flattery (which, it is said, will get you everywhere).

DEALING WITH DIFFICULTIES

IF ALL ELSE FAILS

Now care is clearly necessary here too, flattery is not something to direct at just anyone. But it could be appropriate. Just because *you* would see it as a ploy a million miles off, does not mean that someone else, perhaps actually eager to be thought well of, would not – and maybe your manager or other senior people with whom you deal are like this.

Note: If, when you read in the last paragraph: *Just because you would see it … etc,* you said something to yourself like *Quite right, so I would* – then you have just proved to yourself how well flattery can work.

SUCCESS BREEDS SUCCESS

The senior people you deal with are (probably!) not stupid. They are also motivated in part personally (they want things to go well/have a quiet life, etc). And they know a good thing when they see it.

The ultimate trick to overcome difficulties and get lasting change is to create a thin end of the wedge and **demonstrate** that the change works. It should always be easier to achieve more of the same once they see the advantage.

Example
Say you succeed in your persuasions: something is, reluctantly, delegated to you. Surprise, surprise, all goes well. Perhaps then the next time is viewed differently.

Persuade your manager to try a change, show them that it is a change for the better – and use it as evidence for more of the same.

NOTES

GETTING THE MOST
FROM JOB APPRAISALS

*He who does not seek advice is a fool. His folly blinds him
to Truth and makes him evil, stubborn and a danger to his fellow men.*
Kahlil Gibran

GETTING THE MOST FROM JOB APPRAISALS

HOW AM I DOING?

Though this section deals with formal appraisal situations, evaluation takes many forms and some of the issues addressed (eg: dealing with criticism) may be useful on other, less formal, occasions.

Fact: How you progress is, in every sense, largely down to how well you perform; and your manager is responsible for assessing your performance.

Most organisations have an appraisal process (some better than others) and there is only one way to view them – **as an opportunity**.

You **need** to:

- Know how your performance is viewed
- Review and learn from the past
- Seek improvements for the future
- And, perhaps most important of all, to link the whole process to one of active career management and to the (increasing?) satisfaction and rewards you get from your job

To do this you need to **collaborate** with your manager to make your appraisal useful, and **influence** him or her to ensure the appraisal works for you.

WHAT ARE APPRAISALS FOR?

First, you need to understand why the organisation has an appraisal process, apart from the not unimportant reason that employment legislation says it should. This can sometimes mean that appraisal is seen only as a necessary formality; if so you should make it clear that you **want** it to be useful.

Reasons, which should benefit both individual and organisation, include:

- Reviewing individuals' past performance
- Planning their future work and role
- Setting specific individual future goals
- Agreeing and creating individual ownership of such goals
- Identifying development needs and setting up development activity
- On the spot coaching
- Obtaining feedback
- Reinforcing or extending the reporting relationship
- Acting as a catalyst to delegation
- Focusing on longer-term career progression
- Acting motivationally

WHAT ARE APPRAISALS FOR?

The appraisal review may focus on some or all of the points listed on the previous page; they are not mutually exclusive, but the relative emphasis may well vary. The intention through all of the above is to improve existing performance (taking the view that even good performance can often be improved), and make the likelihood of achieving future plans that much greater.

Understand what the organisation regards as most important, and decide what is most important to you.

HOW APPRAISALS CAN HELP YOU

To get the most from your appraisals, set yourself specific objectives under a number of headings:

- Planning how to make positive points about your performance during the period under review
- Being ready to respond to points raised, including negative ones, appropriately
- Projecting the right image
- Reviewing specific work plans for the next period ahead
- Reviewing factors on which success in the future depends
- Identifying the need or desirability for training and development
- Looking ahead to longer-term career development
- Linking discussion to salary and benefits review

Your thinking about all of these needs to be positive. Don't just think broadly about the sort of year it has been overall. You need to have clear intentions regarding what should (or will inevitably) be discussed, and also about **what you can gain from the discussion** immediately and in the future.

GETTING THE MOST FROM JOB APPRAISALS

PREPARING

The first principle – preparation does **not** start just before the meeting. You need to create and maintain a personal 'appraisal file'.

The starting point is the documentation from your last appraisal. From then on you should make a point of collecting into that file copies of documents that have a bearing on your next meeting. These will include:

- A note of any 'significant events'; eg: comments about what was your first presentation, say, or the fact that you spoke at a trade association meeting or joined a significant committee
- Notifications of targets set, progress against them and ultimate results achieved
- A note of any courses you go on (as a minimum file a copy of the course outline and any evaluation form you may have been asked to complete, together with a note of where any résumé notes are to be found)
- Comments made by other people: maybe the M.D. wrote you a letter of congratulations, or a satisfied customer put pen to paper about service you delivered

PREPARING

You could also include any memos, minutes of meetings or other papers that are useful as a record of your activity and outputs.

The idea is not to hoard everything, or spend a long time amassing this information, a note rather than a whole document may well be sufficient. You can sensibly match the information you gather to the topics that you know will feature in your forthcoming review. For example, if you are judged in part on your communications skills, keep some evidence of them.

Remember that this is not solely a *boasting file* containing references to your successes. If things do go wrong, or less well than you had hoped, they may well be subject to review also – this extends the information you can usefully collect.

Such a file makes preparation just before the event easier and more likely to make the appraisal effective.

PREPARING

Now with good information to hand (and no need to rely on memory to produce details from a year back) you can:

- Take the initiative where necessary
- Study the system (for example, making sure you are aware of the areas to be reviewed and ready for them – see following pages)
- Ask for – with good notice – an agenda and details of what is to be discussed
- Prepare responses to specific points (including explaining why some things have not gone well)
- Set yourself specific goals where appropriate (eg: *I will get agreement to attend a course on X in the next three months*).

In addition, always display a constructive attitude to appraisal when you discuss it with your manager (and especially when you ask for anything).

GETTING THE MOST FROM JOB APPRAISALS

WHAT WILL BE DISCUSSED?

The formal appraisal system will alert you to the main topics that will be discussed. The following are likely to be the sort of headings under which discussion will be organised.

CHECKLIST: Appraisal form

Reviewing past performance

Agenda: The first questions may be linked to finalising the meeting:
- What do you want to come from this meeting?
- Are there special areas you would like to spend time on? And why?

Job: Here questions focus on the task in hand, both *qualitatively* with questions about what you like, have enjoyed or found satisfying or challenging (or a problem); and *quantitatively* with questions about successes, and results and targets met or missed.

WHAT WILL BE DISCUSSED?

Relationships: Investigating your work in terms of how it interacts with other people (whether peers, subordinates or those elsewhere in the organisation, or outside it, with whom you must work or liaise).

Development: This heading allows a focus on skills: what is needed for the job now, how you rate your skills, and whether there are others which need adding or extending (or which are not currently being utilised).

Personal: An opportunity to think more in terms of feelings: have things been easy or difficult? Would you do things differently if it were possible? Are you being stretched, are you learning or getting into a rut?

Special projects: Some such heading allows specific, or more topical, areas of your work to be discussed.

Make sure you **anticipate** (or ask about) as much as possible and **add** (or ask to have added) other topics which the headings indicate *might* be omitted.

DURING THE MEETING

A few matters are of overriding importance here.

- Your appearance (apart from being smartly turned out for an important occasion – your boss's boss may sit in – make sure you look well prepared and unflustered)
- Your manner (always constructive, take your time, do not be rushed and give considered comments and responses)
- The procedure (your manager may have to abide by certain practices as much as you do; while a system is in force, respect it)
- Listen, as in LISTEN! – and make notes as necessary (ask for a second or two to note things down if necessary)
- Stay objective – appraisal is important for all concerned. It will not help to lose your cool and a calm, considered and objective approach throughout is best

During any appraisal meeting the appraisee – you – should do most of the talking; conducting yourself on this basis is good sense.

DURING THE MEETING
YOUR OWN COMMUNICATION

Communication is not the easiest thing in the world, so be sure to keep things working well in such a meeting. Particularly:

- Ensure you are clear (planning helps here)
- Be descriptive (this is no place for saying – *Well, basically it was sort of difficult* – when what is necessary is a clear statement of the situation you faced)
- Concentrate on the **implications of things** and the **results** rather than the detail
- Offer proof of things if they might be contentious (and that means something **other** than you saying *I'm sure*)

Last but by no means least, never let anything go by that you are unclear about – if you are not sure what is being said: **ask**.

> *I know that you understand what you think I said, but I'm not sure you realise that what you heard is not what I meant.*
> The late U.S. President Richard Nixon

FOLLOW UP ACTION

Now the meeting is over what do you do? (Sigh with relief and pour yourself a stiff drink?) Actually, several things:

- Take note of advice given (you might just have lessons to learn, indeed a good boss should make sure you have)
- Request written confirmation (this may be normal, but make sure you get both a summary of the meeting and a specific note of items agreed – it could be best to take the initiative on some of this)
- Take any actions promised and remind, if necessary, of action that your manager has promised (perhaps to have another meeting to take some matter further or to involve you in a specific project)
- Link to your records and planning for the next session, even if this is a year ahead (in some organisations it may be more often) – it is a rolling process

Use – and profit from – the outputs of your appraisal throughout the year.

DEALING WITH CRITICISM

Any appraisal is going to discuss difficulties – it goes with the territory – and you must be ready to deal with this. Three intentions should be paramount, beyond a general desire to put the best complexion on everything.

1. Achieving accuracy:

Here you need to ensure that the right facts are considered. Beware the appraiser using vague statements like *You're never on time with anything*. This is unlikely to be true. But what **are** you late with and what are the implications? It is easier to discuss specifics and questions may well be the route to identify them.

Never argue with anything but the true facts. Checking what is really meant is the first step to responding to what is said in the right way.

DEALING WITH CRITICISM

2. Giving an impression of objectivity:

Do not simply become defensive, or discussion is unlikely to be constructive. Using an acknowledgement of the criticism to position what follows is always useful. It:
- indicates you feel there is a point to discuss (if you do not, then we are back to achieving accuracy – see earlier)
- shows that you are not going to argue unconstructively
- makes it clear that you intend to respond in a serious and considered fashion
- gives you a moment to think (which may be very useful!) and sets up the subsequent discussion so that you can handle it better.

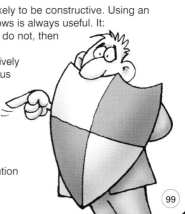

Just a few words may be all that is necessary here. Starting with a yes gives it power – *Yes, there was a problem with that* – and sounds right, even if your intention is to go on to minimise the problem.

99

DEALING WITH CRITICISM

3. Dealing with the points raised:

Now the job is to deal with the matter. Mechanistically, the options are few and therefore manageable. You may need to explain why a difficulty occurred, if so there are four routes to handling things:

1) *Remove the difficulty:* if you can, explain that what seemed like a difficulty or error was not. A delay, say, was not in the original plan, but caused no problem.

2) *Reduce the difficulty:* acknowledge a difficulty, but explain that it was of little significance.

3) *Turn the difficulty into a plus:* sometimes you can argue that what might initially seem like a problem is in fact not. A delay to the original plan might have been allowed for a positive reason – the real problem would have occurred **without** the delay.

DEALING WITH CRITICISM

3. Dealing with the points raised (continued):

4) *Agree the difficulty*: after all, there is no point trying to argue that black is white. Most ordinary mortals have some problems during a whole year of activity. Your job is not to persuade the appraiser that there were **no** problems, but that, on balance, your year was a good one.

The prime purpose of appraisal is to set the scene for successful work in the **coming** year, not argue about what cannot be changed. No one can turn the clock back, but we can all learn from experience. So the key thing to include when the discussion touches on difficulties are the lessons that have been learned for the **future**.

DEALING WITH CRITICISM

The list of implications and actions here is considerable. For instance, failure may have come about because:

- There were unforeseen circumstances (and new procedures are necessary in case such circumstances occur again)

- You may be starting to require skills not previously necessary in the job (and training may be needed to add them quickly to your portfolio)

- You may have made a simple slip (and only need to make a firm mental note not to let it repeat)

There will be lessons to learn, but ultimately the emphasis needs to be on what happens next, and this allows a return to the most constructive elements of the dialogue.

Dealing with criticism constructively allows negative matters to be put on one side and again allows you to take an initiative in managing your manager.

SUMMARY

If you don't believe, you can't achieve.
Proverb

KEY ISSUES

Overall, managing upwards is something that takes place *through* other things that are going on rather than being an activity in its own right.

For example, in communications, projects and meetings you may need to add an element of activity into the process that manages the situation as well as the circumstance.

By and large, what you want is going to help you do your job better – and that is what your boss wants, so there is no inherent clash. Some managers can undeniably be difficult, cussed sometimes, but many problems are more to do with circumstances (eg: lack of time) than to radically opposed views.

Overall, it may help to view the process as *educational*. You are helping them to do the right things rather than seeing it as a more adversarial process.

LOOKING AHEAD

At the end of the day, managing your boss is a full time occupation. It must be done in parallel with the job of doing your job, and getting the results you want (and that your boss wants). It requires – necessitates – a range of skills, particularly in various forms of communication. It also demands patience, persistence and assertiveness; and it needs care and consideration.

Your objectives are essentially twofold (and they overlap) to:

- Ensure you can do your job effectively – with excellence – and achieve, or exceed, your targets

- Enhance your satisfaction from the job and the career progress you make towards new challenges

Getting it right can make the difference between having just a job, and a career that rewards and satisfies; and it can ultimately benefit your boss too. It is not always easy – so remember:

Always do exactly what your boss would do
– if, that is, they knew what they were talking about!
Anon

105

About the Author

Patrick Forsyth
Patrick runs Touchstone Training & Consultancy, an independent
firm specialising in work in marketing, sales and management
and communications skills. With more than 20 years' experience
as a consultant, he has worked in a variety of industries and in
countries worldwide. His training involves one-to-one tutorials,
in-company and public seminars, and also speaking at
business conferences.

He is the author of several pocketbooks, including *The Starting
in Management Pocketbook* and others on meetings, sales and negotiation.
He has also written many other management books including *Successful Time
Management* (Kogan Page) and *Kickstart your Corporate Survival* (Wiley). His books
appear in 22 languages. Additionally, he writes articles for a variety of business journals
and creates corporate publications.

Contact
Patrick may be contacted at:
Touchstone Training & Consultancy, 28 Saltcote Maltings, Maldon, Essex CM9 4QP, UK.
Tel/fax: 01621-859300. E-mail: patrick@touchstonetc.freeserve.co.uk

THE MANAGEMENT POCKETBOOK SERIES

Pocketbooks

Appraisals
Assertiveness
Balance Sheet
Business Planning
Business Writing
Career Transition
Challengers
Coaching
Communicator's
Competencies
Controlling Absenteeism
Creative Manager's
C.R.M.
Cross-cultural Business
Cultural Gaffes
Customer Service
Decision-making
Developing People
Discipline
Diversity
E-commerce
E-customer Care
Emotional Intelligence

Employment Law
Empowerment
Energy and Well-being
Facilitator's
Handling Complaints
Icebreakers
Impact & Presence
Improving Efficiency
Improving Profitability
Induction
Influencing
International Trade
Interviewer's
I.T. Trainer's
Key Account Manager's
Leadership
Learner's
Manager's
Managing Budgets
Managing Cashflow
Managing Change
Managing Upwards
Managing Your Appraisal

Marketing
Meetings
Mentoring
Motivation
Negotiator's
Networking
People Manager's
Performance Management
Personal Success
Presentations
Project Management
Problem Behaviour
Problem Solving
Quality
Resolving Conflict
Sales Excellence
Salesperson's
Self-managed Development
Starting In Management
Stress
Succeeding at Interviews
Teamworking
Telephone Skills

Telesales
Thinker's
Time Management
Trainer Standards
Trainer's
Training Evaluation
Training Needs Analysis
Vocal Skills

Pocketsquares

Great Training Robbery
Hook Your Audience

Pocketfiles

Trainer's Blue Pocketfile of
Ready-to-use Exercises

Trainer's Green Pocketfile of
Ready-to-use Exercises

Trainer's Red Pocketfile of
Ready-to-use Exercises

ORDER FORM

Your details

Name _____

Position _____

Company _____

Address _____

_____

_____

Telephone _____

Fax _____

E-mail _____

VAT No. (EC companies) _____

Your Order Ref _____

Please send me:

	No. copies
The Managing Upwards Pocketbook	☐
The _____ Pocketbook	☐
The _____ Pocketbook	☐
The _____ Pocketbook	☐
The _____ Pocketbook	☐

Order by Post

MANAGEMENT POCKETBOOKS LTD
LAUREL HOUSE, STATION APPROACH, ALRESFORD,
HAMPSHIRE SO24 9JH UK

Order by Phone, Fax or Internet

Telephone: +44 (0)1962 735573
Facsimile: +44 (0)1962 733637
E-mail: sales@pocketbook.co.uk
Web: www.pocketbook.co.uk

Customers in USA should contact:
Stylus Publishing, LLC, 22883 Quicksilver Drive,
Sterling, VA 20166-2012
Telephone: 703 661 1581 or 800 232 0223
Facsimile: 703 661 1501 E-mail: styluspub@aol.com